Smoking Roses

Alyssa Carlston

BookLeaf Publishing
India | USA | UK

Presentation by *BookLeaf Publishing*

Web: www.bookleafpub.com

E-mail: info@bookleafpub.com

ISBN : 978-93-5744-313-5

First edition 2022

DEDICATION

For those who have experienced similar things as I have. You are not alone and we are stronger together. Let your voice be heard.

ACKNOWLEDGEMENT

Thank you to my lover, who has picked up my pieces more times than I can count. Who has proved to me that good people can love me for who I am, despite my many flaws. Who has offered his endless support throughout my mental health journey.

Thank you to all of my friends, who have been there every step of the way, and comforted me in my darkest moments. Who tell me when I'm wrong and help educate me rather than leave me. Who have become my chosen family. Who have my back no matter what.

Thank you to those who have done me wrong. You have made me who I am today. Despite you breaking me and tearing me apart; I am stronger than who I was then, and you can't hurt me anymore.

PREFACE

To anyone who was able to see my art piece in college, I hope you will also be able to appreciate this collection. I hope you get to read my little easter egg.

Trigger Warning: Sexual harassment, rape, manipulation, suicide, and everything in between.

SHE Part 2

She told him

"NO"

But he kept going

She was in love with him

So she thought

"It's okay"

It Was Never Fun

He touched her
in a way no one had before

He touched her
and made her feel like his queen

He touched her
it felt like pure ecstasy

He touched her

He touched her
and she startled

He touched her
and she shook like a leaf

He touched her
but it wasn't fun anymore

He touched her
in a place no one could hear her plea

He touched her
while she was deep in sleep

He touched her
and couldn't wait to   r e l e a s e

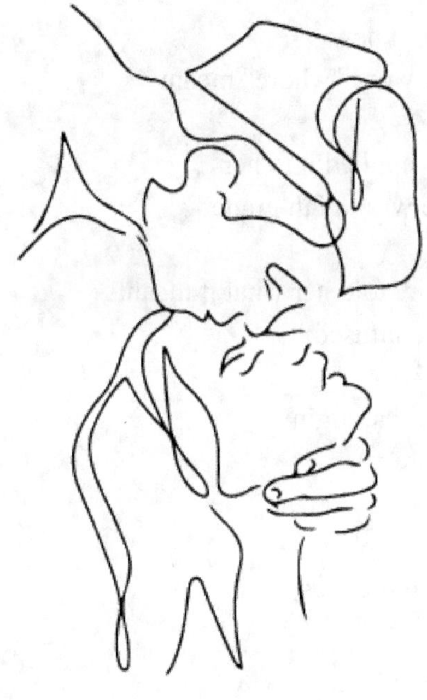

It Started With Him

She never knew
what the word "whore" meant

But they applied it to her
once she was in 8th grade

When they told her what it meant
she was confused

How could a virgin
be a whore

The word spread
and so did her legs

She never did
want to be this way

It was manipulation

It was coercion

It was Rape.

Contradiction

1. Rumors

    turn into truths

2. Will

    crumbles and rebuilds

3. Kill

    the fragility you once knew

4. You

    are the only fighting force

Rumours

Product Usage

It started with

one

And again with

two

She took it to

three

And then to

four

Multiplied it by

five

Until she realized

It only took

one

This Is Love?

Could she go out?

Not without him.

Could she come, too?

Not with him.

Could she see her friends?

They're bad influences.

Could she see her cousin?

She'll turn into a whore
if she's with her.

Could she wear this outfit?

She looks like the queen
of sluts.

Could she dress up?

Only for him.

Could she dress comfortably?

> She's a lazy piece of
shit.

Could she eat this?

> She'll look like a pig.

Could he touch her?

> He's going to anyway.

Could he please stop?

> But her body is telling
him yes.

The Rape Of Her

Run a finger down
She feels like Aphrodite

Drop it in her drink
She acts like Dionysus

Take what he wants
She moves like Persephone

Wake the next day
She thinks like Athena

At first, she's floored
She cries like Demeter

Years harden her
Now she feels like Aries

All because he
Was her Apollo

She Never Stood A Chance

She didn't smoke
Until she inhaled his fumes

He poisoned her brain
Like pesticides in a garden

As everything crumbled to dust
She was left to wither

The single wilted lily
In his plot of smoking roses

Unseen Scars

No no
Don't touch her there

He took it from her
And told her what to wear

She can't stand the feeling
Of wandering hands

Her own body
Feels like foreign lands

She can't find her mind
It has been lost for years

What she thought was wonderland
Was filled with dread and tears

Never Believe Yourself

She still thinks about it
How he tormented her
She could never believe
A person could actually
Be so selfish

This isn't PTSD
No
This is something else
She doesn't have night terrors
But daylight nightmares

Her body image is ruined
Her self-esteem at an all time
L
O
W
Her confidence is nowhere
To be seen

She's tried to have
Good relationships
But no matter how hard
She tries
She's reminded that
There is something wrong with her

And it's her fault

Forever Nightmare

Her head pounds
At the thought of him

The thumping rings in her ears
It's the sound of that night

She has trouble sleeping
She can't drown out the noise

Her eyes shut in the dark
But she still sees what's happening

She usually wonders
Maybe if she was stronger

Things could have gone differently
But they didn't

They could have been happy
But they weren't

She could have shouted
Or screamed
But instead
She cried herself silently to sleep

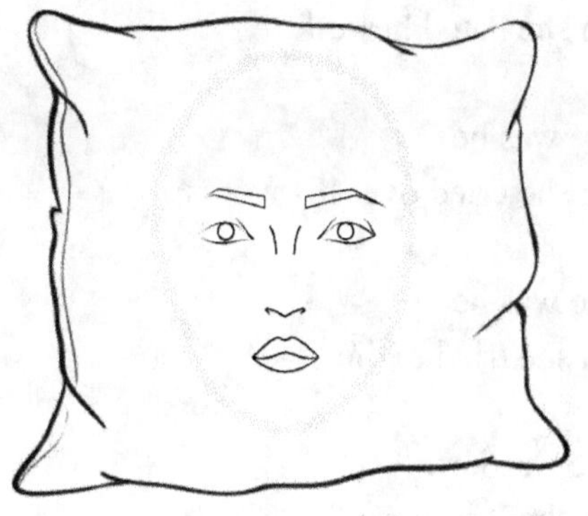

In Her Bed

Where was he
When she felt alone

Where was he
When she hated herself

Where was he
When she cried over his words

Where was he
When she tried to die

Where was he
When she lost herself

Where was he
When she fell asleep

Where was he
When she told him "NO"

He was there
But not the way she wanted

One By One

She just started to blossom
When she was deflowered

Her lily was in full bloom
When her petals were plucked

He loves her
He loves her not

He loves her
He loves her not

He loves her
He loves her not

He uses her
He uses her not

He uses her
He uses her not

He uses her

And her garden
Burned to the ground

The Moment

He dedicated countless
Country love songs to her

One of his many
Manipulation tactics

He would leave her
Then com back to her

He'd make her jealous
On purpose

He up and left the state
And wrote many letters

Then he had the audacity
To write his own tragedy

In one of the letters
He asked her to marry him

Something clicked
She finally snapped

She wasn't brainwashed
Anymore

She left for good

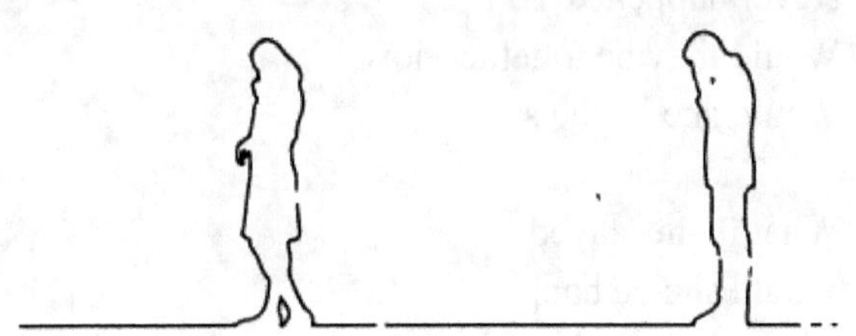

Time Travel

What if they never dated
Would she love herself more
Would she be broken again
By someone else

What if that night
Never happened
Would they be together now
Would she be the same

What if she stayed
Would she be happy
Would he treat her better
Or would he get angrier

What if he never asked
To marry her
Would they still talk
Would she have left still

What if she could go back
Would she want to change
How everything went
Would she go back at all

What if

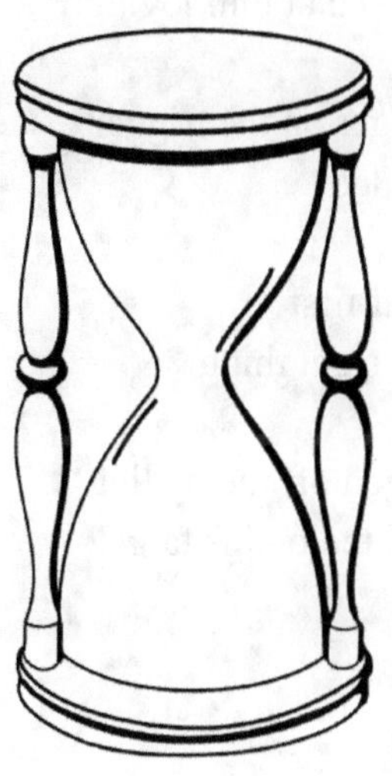

For Now

He loaded his weapon
When she minded her business

Aimed down the sight
When she looked at him lovingly

Placed his finger on the trigger
When she smiled

He hesitated at first
Unsure of the right thing

But he shrugged off the feeling
And concentrated on his target

He fired

BOOM

BOOM

BOOM

And everything was quiet

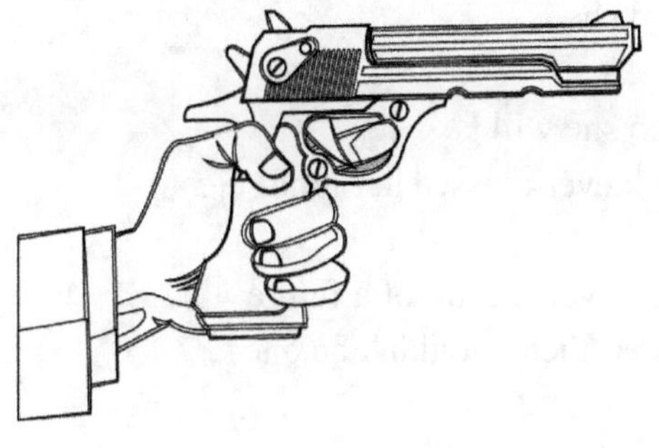

Mental Note

She sat by herself
Talking with her reflection

Wondering of who she was
Who she is

Who she will be
Has never crossed her mind

She never dreamt of a future
In fear there wouldn't be one

What is she to do now
Dream of an end goal

That's not how this works
Depression is funny that way

She's stuck in the past
Not focused on the present

Self-deprecation is key
For her to cope

But as the saying goes:

Every great artist
Has an even greater struggle

It Was Just A Game

A game
Of Cat and Mouse

A game
Of Hide and Seek

A game
Of Red Rover

A game
Of Dodgeball

A game
Of Touch-And-Go

A game
Of Red Light Green Light

A game
Of Firetruck

And firetrucks don't stop
For red lights

Never Grow Up

Mentally
She was still a child
Who had her innocence taken

She's mentally matured
Since that night
Which most think is good

What people see
Is someone who's 23
Acting older than her age

She's been complimented
Since she was 19
Saying she wasn't like most girls

But behind that closed door
She longs to be a child
All over again

She collects stuffed animals
And enjoys everything soft
While playing comforting games

Time flies
And so does she

When she's dreaming
Of her childhood fantasies

Growth

She slowly started
To find herself
After that despicable man

She focused on herself
And slowly healed
By confronting her demons

She made art
About him
Minus the victim blame

The one true time
She let herself be angry
And let herself cry

All of her feelings
On a canvas
Are now her pride and joy

She pours her heart
Out on these pages
Her blood sweat and tears

In the words of AJR
She may not be happy yet

But she's way less sad

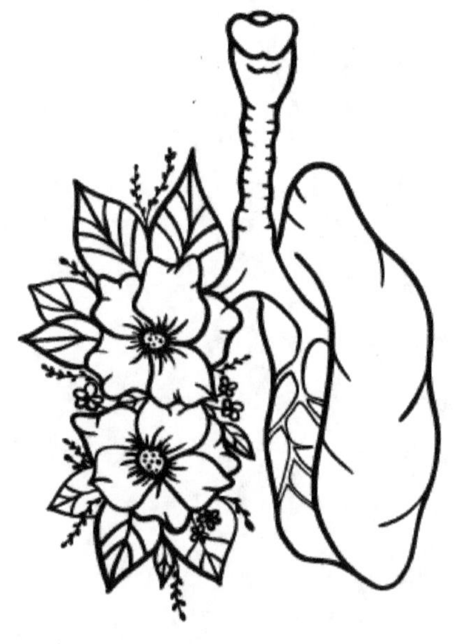

But You Did

Flowers couldn't save her

Chocolates couldn't save her

Jewelry couldn't save her

Date nights couldn't save her

Family couldn't save her

Solitude couldn't save her

Therapy couldn't save her

She couldn't save herself

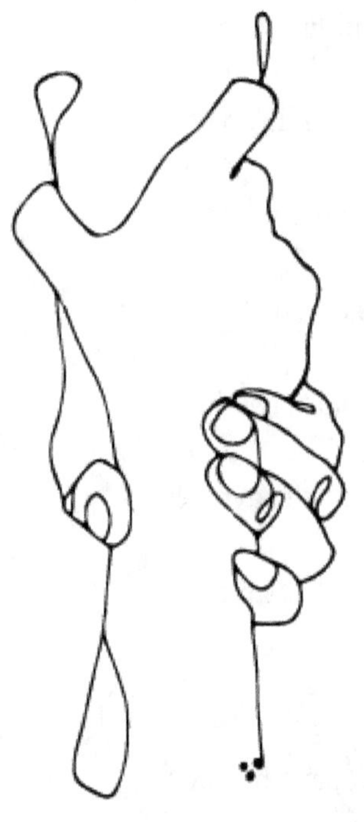

9 789357 443135